GREAT GUSTS

WINDS OF THE WORLD
AND THE SCIENCE BEHIND THEM

poems by
MELANIE CROWDER
and **MEGAN BENEDICT**

illustrated by
KHOA LE

mit Kids Press

Can you ever really *see* the wind?

Look to the trees, rustling
beneath a songbird's wing, gusting
on a spitting, rainy day, blustering

or high above
where clouds are
tugged
across
the sky
by an invisible hand.

Hints,
footprints left behind.

Can you ever really *know* the wind?

Lift your face to the breeze—
let it bathe your cheeks
sift through your hair
tease your fingertips.

        Listen
while the wind whispers
its name.

Bull's-Eye Squall

On a clear, fine day
you might spot a cloud,
crisp and bright,
small and white.

As it draws near
the air rushes and curls—
updrafts and downdrafts,
swirling-around drafts.

Off the coast of South Africa, **updrafts**
and **downdrafts** can combine to create tornado-like forces called nautical **squalls**.
As the warm updrafts rise, they collect moisture from the air and form a small white cloud cap,
which looks like a bull's-eye and acts as a visual marker of these extreme windstorms.

The wild wind circles,
spinning a target.
Stealthy, it forms
an invisible storm.

Born on the waves,
a tornado takes aim—
twisting, whip-curling,
then listing, unfurling.

A bull's-eye squall
begins with a cloud cap

so

so

small.

Katabatic

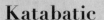

Floating above the polar plateau
is the coldest air you'll ever know.

It spills across the frozen plain
but squeezed
　　　then squished
　　　　　and squeezed again

Antarctica's ice-covered polar plateau cools the air above it. That cold, dense air
sinks downslope toward the sea, over rugged ice and mountains, which funnel
and speed up the descending air, creating intense winds.

the katabatic winds, they roar,
picking up speed, nearing the shore.

Blustering over wave and floe,
the strongest winds you'll ever know!

Oroshi

Down the mountain's flank,
winter's great gust warns: not yet,
eager blossom. Wait.

The oroshi of Japan is a strong
winter wind that drives down mountain
slopes. This wind sculpts trees in its path, both
those growing naturally in the landscape and ones
planted as windbreaks to provide shelter for homes
in the region.

Maestro

Off Italy's western coast
the maestro sweeps the air.

A fine summer day
to dance and play,
he swaggers and slides,
gestures and glides.

Who could find fault
in a maestro so fair?

During the summer months, this warm northwesterly wind blows persistently over Italy. The maestro is an **anabatic**, or upward, **sea breeze** that brings fair weather from the Mediterranean during the day and dies down during the night when the air temperature above land drops.

When a cold, northeasterly winter wind meets the warmer air over Lake Michigan, it picks up moisture, causing snowstorms. Chicago has long been known as the Windy City, in part because it's close to the polar **jet stream**, but it wasn't until musician Lou Rawls called the city's biting wind the "hawk" in his 1967 song "Dead End Street" that the name stuck.

The Hawk

Swoop, dive, flit, skim
from the chilly shores of Lake Michigan
past crowded streets, architectural feats
    an icy blast,
      fierce wingbeats—
Chicago's winter wind.

Buran

Out on the steppe

where sky abounds
unspooling white all around—

a winter wind blows   billows of snow,
billows that heave and grow.

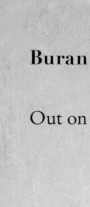

Inside the blizzard

          wind whips and whirls,
          howls and hurls—

              a storm so bright,   a storm so white,
              a storm to steal your sight.

While the buran blows year-round, blizzards make it more brutal in winter. Vast grasslands stretching from eastern Europe across Russia and into China allow this wind to blow unhindered for days at a time.

Sudestada

Beware—

In Argentina, the south winds blow
where waters twine, combine, and flow:
      one silver river to the ocean.

From Uruguay, the swift air stirs,
circles east with rain and spurs
      unbridled waves on the ocean.

The vessels, caught when it quickly rounds,
rock and twist, capsize and drown:
      shipwrecks on the floor of the ocean.

As wind from the Pacific Ocean hits the peaks of the Andes Mountains, it is forced south toward the Atlantic, where it joins the **high-pressure system** over the Río de la Plata estuary—the mouth of the river. When that high-pressure system meets a **low-pressure system** over Uruguay, the winds merge, then howl north, creating sudestadas, which whip the waters of the estuary back toward land, causing shipwrecks and major flooding in Argentina, Uruguay, and even Brazil.

Squamish

In the far Northwest,
where peaks graze the sky
and water runs wild through the land,
the wind howls, angry,
funnels through fjords
chasing, diving, ripping
polar air pushing
against its mountainous confines
                    until . . .
out on the sea
it's free.

The Squamish is an intense **gap wind** that flows out through the fjords of British Columbia over the coastal waters of the Pacific Ocean. It's caused by an arctic **weather system** with **anticyclonic** winds that form over Alaska and Canada in winter. These winds can reach hurricane force and bring blizzard conditions.

Willy-willy

A little hot air
rising too fast
     sends you spinning
        kicking up dust
   whirling, willy-nilly
out of control.

Suck in a breath,
cool and calm—
    let that grit   go.

An Australian dust devil is sometimes called a willy-willy. Most of Australia is arid and receives very little rain. In this dry, sparse environment, high surface temperatures warm the air, making it spin upward in strong **updrafts**. This rotation causes the willy-willy to move across the landscape; when it reaches an area of cooler surface air, the funnel collapses.

Helm

You'll hear it first,
the rumbling roar
across the damp
and wild moor.
The clouds will bank
on craggy fell,
down rugged land
the wind will swell
and sweep across
the heath and hill—
a shroud of clouds,
a ghostly chill.
Across the damp
and wild moor
lay cairns to mark
the rumbling roar.

This dry, downslope **foehn** wind is the only named wind in Britain. When northeasterly winds whip over the Pennine mountain range in northern England, a cloud bank (called the helm cloud) catches atop the peaks. Once the wind reaches the valley below, the air spirals up and down, forming a long, cylindrical cloud (called the helm bar).

Moani

Far out to sea
sailors raise their heads,
close their eyes,
                b r e a t h e

as the wind wanders by,
bearing sweet smells:

> hala, ʻōhiʻa
> lehua, maile
>
> flowering pine, fiery
> blossoms, fragrant vine.

The heady scent
beckons the travelers
home.

This **land breeze** gathers the scent of the tropical plants in the Puna region of Hawai'i, then wafts the fragrance over the open ocean; travelers sometimes smell the island before they see it. These islands feature complex wind systems due to their positioning on the open ocean, geographical features such as mountains, valleys, and channels between islands, as well as the frequent presence of the **trade winds**. Ancestral understanding of the many local winds of Hawai'i has been passed down through oral tradition.

Sumatra Squall

The storm arrives before the sun.
A line of thunderclouds
breaks the sky—

a marching band
whistling through the gap
between land and sea.

BOOM. *Clash!* Swoosh-thwack.
BOOM. *Clash!* Whish-whack.

Finally, gentle rain,
a steady drum—*rat-a-tat-tat*
sounds the retreat—*pitter-pitter-pat.*

As night winds gust off the mountains on the island of Sumatra and meet the warmer, moist air over the Strait of Malacca, thunderclouds sometimes form and combine into **a squall line.** These powerful storms roll over Malaysia and Singapore in the predawn hours, bringing strong winds, downpours, and percussive thunder and lightning shows.

Papagayo Jet

Even fierce, howling winds bring
hope, remake this world.
Rest, fragile beasts, where algae
blooms in cooling swirls.

A **gap wind**, the Papagayo jet originates in the Caribbean Sea, is funneled through a pass in the Cordillera mountains in Nicaragua, then blows across the Gulf of Papagayo. This powerful southeast wind whips up the warm waters around the equator in **cyclonic** and **anticyclonic** directions, stirring up deeper, cooler waters and helping to maintain the **Costa Rica Thermal Dome**, a crucial ecosystem for many threatened and endangered species.

Ghibli

The planet turns
and the skies respond,
the oceans, too, in spinning gyres.

This tilt and twirl bends the winds, sends
hot air down to the desert floor,
then lashing out, roiling
over rolling dunes,
churning toward the sea.

The waters
slow the winds
as the coast draws near.
Sandy rain splatters over olive groves
and vineyards, down slippery slides
and seesaws, over watched window panes.

The planet turns;
a blood rain falls
once the desert meets the sea.

The planet turns;
the oceans respond,
the wind, too,

        and you
        and me.

The ghibli, from Libya, is one of several **sirocco** winds, which come from the **high-pressure system** above the Sahara, in northern Africa. Because the desert air is so hot, as this dry, sand-laden wind crosses the Mediterranean Sea, it can pick up lots of moisture. Blowing humid air across southern Europe, it can sometimes produce a red rain, or "blood rain," as a mixture of sand and water fall from the sky.

What Makes the Wind?

~⌒

Wind is air in motion.

The sun heats the earth and the air above it, but not equally. Geographic features like mountains and oceans, and even factors such as the angle of sunlight, can change how hot air gets. Air moves in response to temperature changes. Cold air sinks because its atoms and molecules slow down and squeeze together, building pressure and making the air more dense and heavy. Warm air rises because its atoms and molecules move faster and spread out, releasing pressure and making the air lighter.

Imagine the moment when you're let out for recess. Classmates scatter in different directions rather than staying clustered together. Air works like that too—it wants to spread out to fill empty space. Air moves from high-pressure areas to low-pressure areas. That moving air is wind! It speeds up, slows down, twists, and turns when it interacts with things such as landforms, cityscapes, bodies of water, and even the Earth's rotation.

How Are Winds Named?

When a wind blows the same way in the same place long enough to become familiar to the people who live there, it sometimes earns its own name. These names might reflect the wind's effect on weather or temperature or tell us how ferociously the wind blows or if it brings rain, snow, or sand. Other wind names are based in culture, myth, or even our five senses.

Are there local winds you've come to know? What name would you give the wind?

Local Poetic Traditions

Like the winds, forms of poetry are as unique as the regions where they originate. While most of the poems in this book are written in free verse, a few follow traditional patterns. "Oroshi" is a haiku, a kind of Japanese poetry that consists of three lines in a 5-7-5 syllabic pattern. "Helm" is written in iambs (unstressed-stressed metric beats that sound like *ba-BUM*) as a nod to the iambs that make up English sonnets. Finally, "Papagayo Jet" is written as a copla, a form used in the folk poetry of Central and South America. Coplas are usually sung and consist of linked stanzas. While the form can vary greatly, "Papagayo Jet" is one four-line stanza in a 7-5-7-5 syllabic pattern.

Where the Winds Blow

1 **Bull's-Eye Squall:** South Africa

2 **Katabatic:** Antarctica

3 **Oroshi:** Japan

4 **Maestro:** Italy

5 **The Hawk:** Illinois, United States

6 **Buran:** Russia

7 **Sudestada:** Argentina & Uruguay

8 **Squamish:** British Columbia, Canada

9 **Willy-willy:** Australia

10 **Helm:** England

11 **Moani:** Hawai'i, United States

12 **Sumatra Squall:** Malaysia & Singapore

13 **Papagayo Jet:** Nicaragua & Costa Rica

14 **Ghibli:** Libya

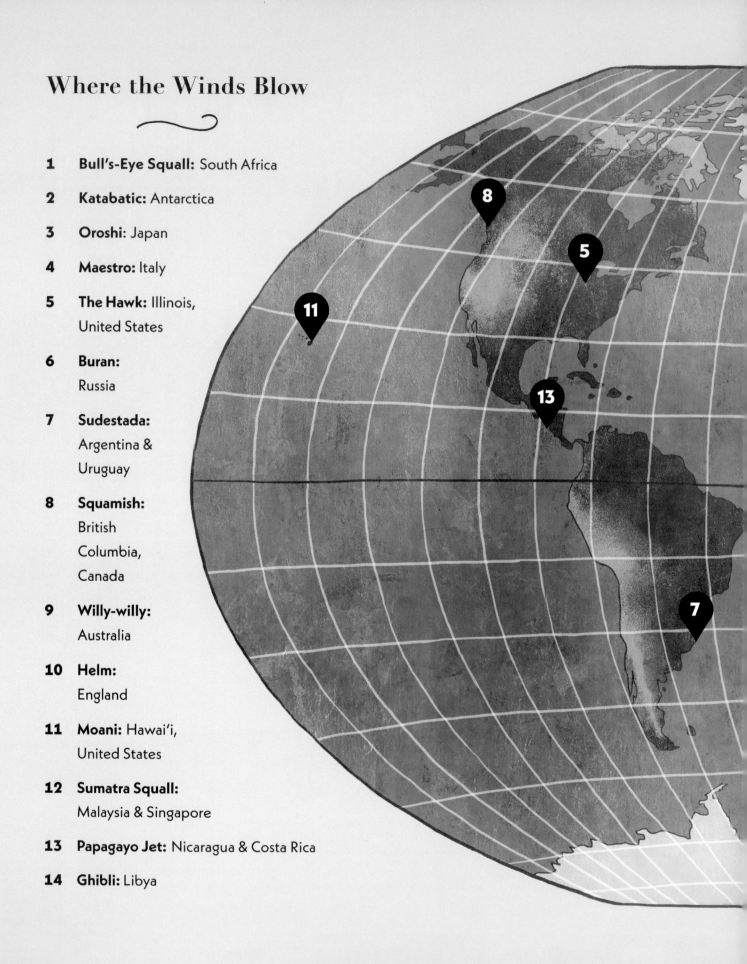

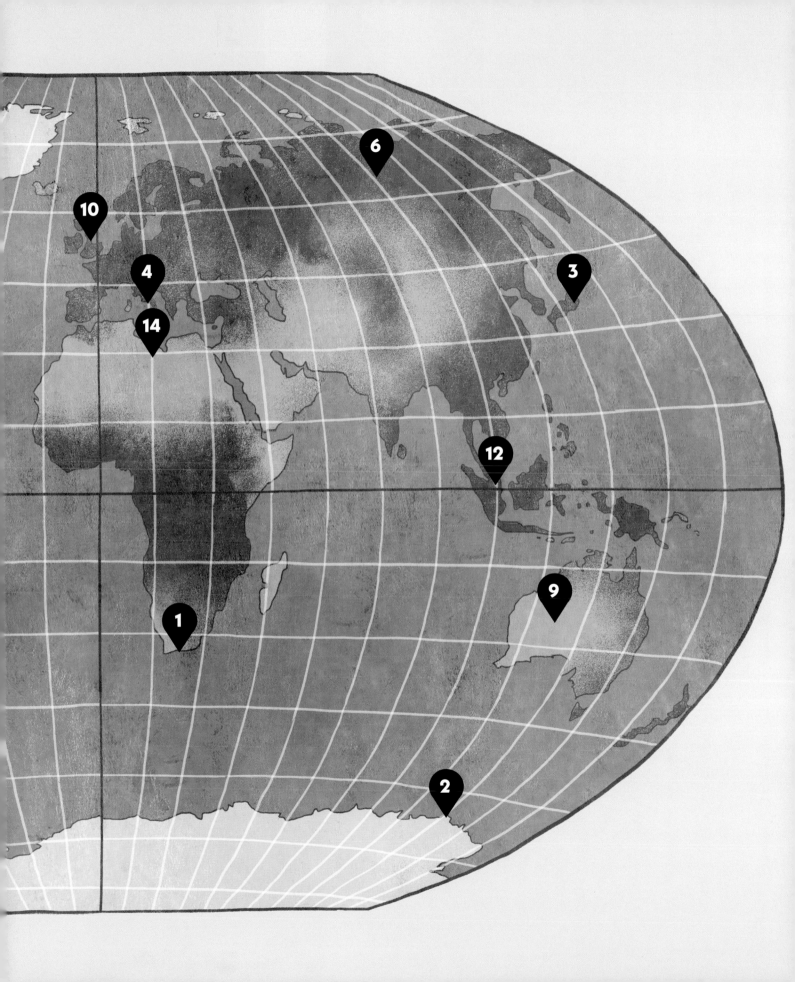

Glossary

anabatic: a kind of wind that moves upward

anticyclonic: turning clockwise in the Northern Hemisphere and counterclockwise in the Southern Hemisphere

Costa Rica Thermal Dome: an area where the Papagayo Jet stirs up cold seawater in the otherwise warm equatorial waters nearly 200 miles (320 kilometers) off the Gulf of Papagayo. The Costa Rica Thermal Dome allows for algae blooms and a diversity of food sources for numerous marine species, including dolphins, jumbo flying squid, sharks, and even endangered blue whales.

cyclonic: turning counterclockwise in the Northern Hemisphere and clockwise in the Southern Hemisphere

downdraft: a downward moving gust of cool air

foehn: a kind of wind that blows downslope and is generally warm and dry

gap wind: a wind that speeds up as it is forced through the spaces between mountains. These winds can reach hurricane-force speeds, exceeding 100 miles (160 kilometers) per hour.

high-pressure system: cool, dry air that turns in an anticyclonic motion, pushing air outward. Because cold air sinks, these systems are known for clear skies since they don't allow moist air to rise and gather into clouds.

jet stream: narrow, strong, fast-moving winds found high in the atmosphere that travel mostly west to east. When rising warm air masses meet sinking cold air masses, air currents form. There are four main jet streams on Earth: two polar and two subtropical.

land breeze: offshore wind that occurs as air over land cools quickly during the night, sinks, and is drawn out to sea to replace the warmer, rising air over the water

low-pressure system: warm, moist air that turns in a cyclonic motion, pulling air into its center. Because warm air rises, often picking up moisture, these systems can form clouds and bring strong winds and storms.

sea breeze: a wind that occurs as air over land warms quickly during the day, rises, and draws cooler air from over the ocean onto land

sirocco: a warm, southerly wind that blows north from the Sahara Desert across the Mediterranean Sea

squall: strong winds that begin and end suddenly and are formed by updrafts and downdrafts. To be considered a squall, a wind must increase its speed by at least 18 miles (29 kilometers) per hour and maintain that speed for more than a minute. Typically, squalls maintain speeds higher than 25 miles (40 kilometers) per hour, can last for several minutes or even hours, and can include rain, hail, snow, lightning, and/or thunder.

squall line: a group of severe thunderstorms that forms in a line and precedes a cold front. The line typically spans 10–20 miles (16–32 kilometers), but some can stretch more than 100 miles (160 kilometers) long.

trade winds: easterly winds to the north and south of the equator that blow consistently due to the Earth's rotation

updraft: a gust of warm air that rises upward

weather system: the movement of air around the globe; high- or low-pressure systems (see definitions on facing page)

For Further Reading

Boyle, Doe. *Hear the Wind Blow*. Illustrated by Emily Paik. Chicago: Albert Whitman, 2021.

Breen, Mark, and Kathleen Friestad. *The Kids' Book of Weather Forecasting: Build a Weather Station, "Read" the Sky & Make Predictions!* Nashville, TN: Williamson, 2008.

Dorros, Arthur. *Feel the Wind*. New York: Crowell, 1989.

Drimmer, Stephanie Warren. *National Geographic Kids Ultimate Weatherpedia: The Most Complete Weather Reference Ever*. Washington, DC: National Geographic, 2019.

Sherman, Josepha. *Gusts and Gales: A Book About Wind*. Illustrated by Omarr Wesley. Minneapolis: Picture Window Books, 2004.

MELANIE CROWDER teaches at Vermont College of Fine Arts and is the author of nine acclaimed books for young readers. Her titles have received numerous starred reviews, as well as national and state awards, including having been named a *Kirkus Reviews* Best Young Adult Book of the Year, a YALSA Best Fiction for Young Adults selection, and a New York Public Library Best Book for Kids. Her historical novel in verse, *Audacity*, received a *Bulletin of the Center for Children's Books* Blue Ribbon and the Jefferson Cup. She lives on the Colorado Front Range, where downslope chinook winds regularly visit her home.

MEGAN BENEDICT holds an MFA in Writing for Children and Young Adults from Vermont College of Fine Arts. Her poetry has been published in *Bravery* magazine and the *Hyacinth Review*. *Great Gusts* is her first picture book. She writes poetry and fiction in the foothills of the Colorado Rocky Mountains and loves to chase the salty sea breezes of any coast she can get to.

KHOA LE is the illustrator of numerous picture books, including *Sugar in Milk* by Thrity Umrigar, a *School Library Journal* Best Book of the Year, and *Miriam at the River* by Jane Yolen, an Association of Jewish Libraries Sydney Taylor Honor Book. Khoa Le lives in Ho Chi Minh City, Vietnam, where she works to preserve her country's ocean as a member of a local free-dive group.

For Mom, who taught me to love books by the armful
MC

For Kelby, who dreams with me
MB

For Thu Na
KL

The MIT Press, the ☰mit Kids Press colophon, and MIT Kids Press are trademarks of The MIT Press, a department of the Massachusetts Institute of Technology, and used under license from The MIT Press. The colophon and MIT Kids Press are registered in the US Patent and Trademark Office.

First edition 2024

Library of Congress Catalog Card Number pending
ISBN 978-1-5362-2451-1

23 24 25 26 27 28 CCP 10 9 8 7 6 5 4 3 2 1

Printed in Shenzhen, Guangdong, China

This book was typeset in Stempel Garamond.
The illustrations were created digitally.

MIT Kids Press
an imprint of Candlewick Press
99 Dover Street
Somerville, Massachusetts 02144

mitkidspress.com
candlewick.com